What Others Are Saying

"The pro-life movement is a movement of converts and therefore a movement of hope. There is nothing more unnatural than paying a healer, a doctor, to take the life of a child. Abortion is devastating, and the 'relief' it promises is nowhere to be found in the aftermath. This beautiful book is a finger that points to healing, hope, and freedom that is possible through Jesus Christ. He is the Great Healer, and these pages show His power to restore our brokenness."

—Shawn Carney
CEO and President of 40 Days for Life
Bestselling author of *The Beginning of the End of Abortion*

"Infused with hope and healing on every page. *Planned from the Start* is a beacon of light, love, and restoration for anyone who has experienced the trauma incurred by abortion."

—Robia Scott
Author of *Counterfeit Comforts*
Actress in *Unplanned*

"Breathtaking. I have never cried while previewing a manuscript for endorsement, but I did with *Planned from the Start*. Tears that quickly turned to hope and freedom. If you need healing from a crisis pregnancy, this book is for you. If you know someone who does, this book is your gift to them."

—Laura Harris Smith, CNC
Author of *Get Well Soon, The Healthy Living Handbook*,
and *The 30-Day Faith Detox*; TV host of *the THREE*

"*Planned from the Start* is an incredibly powerful resource for anyone who has experienced the pain that abortion causes. The testimonies and moments of reflection within are a beautiful reminder that God's grace is sufficient for us. I believe that this book will bring healing and restoration to millions."

—Ashley Bratcher
Actress in *Unplanned*

"*Planned from the Start* tackles a very difficult subject with God's grace and kindness that offers a healing path for anyone who has felt the toxic effects of abortion. Lorraine Varela has beautifully compiled this devotional with Scriptures, meditative reflections, and the compelling stories of many who have not only suffered from the traumas of abortion, but those who have also found forgiveness, comfort, and wholeness—with the hope that through this book, you will find the same too. I believe this book will also be a valuable tool for spiritual counselors, pastors, and anyone who seeks to help others in their healing process. As you read, may your heart be healed and your soul made whole."

—Joshua Mills
Bestselling author of *Moving in Glory Realms*

"*Unplanned* powerfully removes blinders regarding the truth of abortion and the value of human life. *Planned from the Start* picks up where the movie leaves off, offering the first step toward healing for women and men who have suffered through the trauma of abortion. This vital resource offers hope as it restores identity, destiny, and purpose."

—Daryl Lefever
Producer of *Unplanned* and *I Can Only Imagine*

"*Planned from the Start* opened up unexpected places in my heart. It beautifully led me through many emotions and brought peace to painful memories. Long-held lies in my mind were replaced with God's truth and His love for me, and I received so much insight and encouragement from the times of reflection. For any woman who has been through the agonizing experience of abortion, this healing devotional by Lorraine Varela will bring comfort and closure to your heart, soul, mind, and body."

—Julie True
Julie True Ministries
Singer, Songwriter, Soaking Worship Music Artist

"In the pages of this masterful work, Lorraine takes us on a journey of pain, loss, grief, restoration, and joy as exemplified in the life of Abby Johnson. Through this beautiful devotional you will see the omnipotence of God in taking broken pieces and shattered dreams and using them for His glory and our good. I recommend this book to any person looking for home in their darkest hour and longing to experience the grace of God in ways they have never imagined. God has a plan even for the unplanned!"

—Dr. Kynan Bridges
Bestselling author of *90 Days of Power Prayer*
Pastor, Speaker

"I know a number of women who've had abortions, and they seem to fall into one of two camps. Either they're still covered in a thick shadow of shame, or, because they've received God's healing and forgiveness, they've found a passion in their souls and have gone on to do brilliant things for God. Oh, I long for every hurting heart to know Christ's unfathomable mercy and grace amid the ashes and wreckage of abortion. My friend, Lorraine, has crafted a beautifully deep devotional that will minister to your heart and lead you to a place of healing you never thought possible. You may fear that you won't survive it. But you'll not only survive it, you will go on to thrive in life! As you pursue your healing, you'll find a Savior waiting with open arms, ready to restore you. Take your time and work your way through the pages of this treasured resource. You'll be glad you did."

—Susie Larson
Author, Show Host, National Speaker

"*Planned from the Start: A Healing Devotional* is a face-to-face encounter with the Healer Himself. The testimonies of hope and restoration in this book will be inspirational to all who read."

—Fabiano Altamura
Co-Producer of *Unplanned*
Dean, Bethel Conservatory of the Arts

PLANNED
FROM THE START
A HEALING DEVOTIONAL

PLANNED
FROM THE START
A HEALING DEVOTIONAL

JOY
FORGIVENESS
GRACE
COMFORT
HOPE

LORRAINE MARIE VARELA

ROMANS 8:28
BOOKS

AN IMPRINT OF REDEMPTION PRESS

Cover design by Jason Pearson/Pearpod.com
Interior photography by Lorraine Marie Varela

Published by Romans 8:28 Books, an imprint of Redemption Press,
PO Box 427, Enumclaw, WA 98022

Toll Free (844) 2REDEEM (273-3336)

Romans 8:28 Books and Redemption Press are honored to present this title in partnership with the author. Romans 8:28 Books and Redemption Press provide our imprint seal representing design excellence, creative content, and high quality production.

ISBN 13: 978-1-7329625-0-7 (Hardcover)
978-1-7329625-2-1 (ePub)
978-1-7329625-1-4 (Mobi)

Library of Congress Catalog Card Number: 2018964396

Contents

CONTENTS

Foreword

IF YOU ARE READING THESE WORDS, it's because you are numbered among the hundreds of thousands of women who have suffered the trauma of abortion. This book is a love letter to you. You are not alone. God cares deeply about your struggle, your pain, and your fight to get beyond the past and move forward into your future.

More than five years ago, while feeding our caffeine addiction at a local coffee shop, we ran into a friend who handed us a copy of Abby Johnson's book *Unplanned* and said, "You need to make this into a film." Not thinking much of it at the time, we agreed to check it out and took the book home. After reading it, we agreed. Abby's story had to be told. With prayerful conviction, we embarked on this wild adventure.

Along the way, we've met many women who have tearfully told us their abortion stories. We began to realize *Unplanned* isn't just about abortion; it's about the aftermath. It's about the pain of women unable to forgive themselves, the pain of women living with hidden guilt and shame, and their struggle to find healing from their pain.

A quick search on the Internet uncovers some sobering statistics:

- 60% of post-abortive women stated that they felt "a part of me died"
- 62% couldn't forgive themselves
- 36% have had thoughts of suicide

Abortion has impacted so many lives. It crosses all socio-economic, racial, and cultural boundaries. The Christian church is no less impacted. More than seventy percent of women electing an abortion claimed a Christian religious preference. Forty-three percent reported attending worship services at their church at least monthly, if not more frequently. In fact, abortion is so widespread that research reveals one in four women will have an abortion by age forty-five.

And yet, no one wants to acknowledge or talk about the emotional pain that comes with abortion.

A few years into this journey, we met Lorraine and Gabriel Varela at a writers' conference where we were the keynote speakers. It was instantly clear that the Lord had placed them in our path. Lorraine introduced herself as a writer who had just been given a contract from a Christian publisher to write a book of prayer strategies. She also shared that, as we were speaking, the Lord prompted her with inspiration for her first screenplay, which we've since purchased for future production. As we were preparing to film *Unplanned*, we invited Lorraine and Gabriel to establish and oversee our on-set ministry team. Lorraine's dedication to intercession for this project and her heart for women, along with her God-inspired writing gift, made her the obvious choice to pen this devotional. As you read the following pages, we are confident you will agree.

Abortion is not the "unpardonable sin." The Lord offers mercy, grace, and forgiveness that leads to the healing and restoration of identity. Our prayer is that this devotional will be the catalyst that begins a personal healing journey for every person who has been affected by abortion. May the Lord use this book to bring healing to you and to those who love you.

—Cary Solomon and Chuck Konzelman
Writers-Directors of *Unplanned*

Introduction

There is no pit so deep that He is not deeper still.
—Betsie ten Boom, Ravensbrück concentration camp prisoner, 1944

ABBY JOHNSON BELIEVED IN GOD. She also believed in helping women in crisis. Unplanned pregnancies brought women through her doors at Planned Parenthood, where she worked as a clinic director. "No one grows up wanting to have an abortion," Abby said. But abortion was legal—and Abby thought legal meant it must be okay.

Abby believed the lies she had been taught about infants in the womb—lies she repeated to women who sought her counsel. "It's not a baby. It's just a clump of tissue." She defended these lies for years, convincing women that the right thing to do was to kill their own children. Then one fateful day, what she saw changed everything—the day she assisted with an ultrasound-guided abortion and watched a thirteen-week-old infant fight for its life. In that moment Abby knew that she had been deceived, too.

Abortion leaves hidden scars that run deep. Both pro-life and pro-choice groups have identified five key areas of common emotional responses that affect women who have undergone one or more abortion procedures: grief, guilt, shame, regret, and depression.

These abortion scars aren't limited to the women alone—men whose fatherhoods have been denied may also find themselves faced with the same emotional challenges, whether they were complicit with facilitating the abortions or not. And the circle grows larger still—mothers or fathers who forced abortions on their daughters, grandparents who never knew their grandchildren, friends who assisted women to the clinics, siblings who lost nieces and nephews, children who lost siblings, and future children whose parents struggle to bond with them. Although often unaware, many experience the heavy weight of abortion trauma.

If you wonder whether abortion trauma is affecting your life, here are some questions that may bring clarity:

- Do you struggle with forgiving yourself—or others—for your abortion?
- Does it seem impossible that God would forgive you?
- Do you feel like you will never be accepted by others?
- Do you experience unexpected flashes of anger or rage?
- Do you feel the need to punish yourself?
- Do you turn to dependency on alcohol, drugs, or food for comfort? Are there other behaviors you engage in to mask your pain?
- Do you struggle to connect with your emotions or to attach emotionally to others?
- Do you feel broken with regret?
- Do you have difficulty concentrating or sleeping? Do flashbacks or nightmares of your abortion cause you distress?
- Do thoughts of suicide or self-hatred plague your mind?

If you answered *yes* to one or more of these questions, know that you are not alone. For every area of pain, the Lord has His antidote of peace.

Where there is grief, He anoints your head with joy.

Where there is guilt, He offers you forgiveness.

Where there is shame, He covers you in grace.

Where there is regret, He wraps you in comfort.

Where there is depression, He lifts your heart with hope.

Through it all, His love restores your identity and renews the destiny He purposed for you from eternity past.

Each section of this devotional addresses one of these core areas of emotional and spiritual pain. They begin with a testimonial of someone who has walked the path of abortion and found healing through the love of God. There is power in testimony! You may identify with these stories through parallels from your own experience. If so, grab hold of the deliverance and freedom offered as you align your heart to receive from the Lord.

Your healing journey continues with devotions to inspire you, providing questions to consider as you pause in reflection and quiet your heart. This is your time for self-evaluation—an internal check-up of areas that have caused you distress, and an opportunity to refine your perspective as you meditate on God's character and heart.

These questions are followed by an intentional time to pause in His presence and listen for His voice. Don't be in a hurry—allow time for the Holy Spirit to minister to you as He instills a greater awareness of His presence and His love. The Lord may remind you of a promise in Scripture. He may speak a thought directly to your heart or bring to your mind a visual picture of His love for you. He is a creative God who desires to encounter you and make Himself known. You are encouraged to use the pages of this devotional to write down your own thoughts *and* the impressions He places on your heart.

Enter into this time with expectation, and trust that God will speak and minister to you in your place of need. Listening to God's voice may be new or unfamiliar to you. You may need to overcome barriers of doubt, fear, or frustration before you can receive from Him. *Doubt* is a barrier of the mind that interferes with your ability to recognize God's voice. *Fear* is a barrier the enemy uses to destroy your faith. *Frustration* is a barrier that threatens to drain your hope and steal your joy.

Recognize the barriers that hold you back. Ask the Lord to show you what He wants you to know. Jesus said, "My sheep hear My voice" (John 10:27 NKJV). You can trust that He will speak to you, and you *will* hear Him. His voice is gentle and kind. You will be able to discern His voice from the accuser who wants to keep you bound in guilt and shame—the accuser who says that forgiveness applies to everyone else, *but not you*. The accuser is a liar. You've listened to the enemy's lies long enough. It's time for a change.

Healing is a process that the Lord walks with you in love. His heart is for you. His love surrounds you. May this devotional help your healing journey to begin, leading you into renewed identity, destiny, and purpose God planned for you before He laid the foundation of the world. He rejoices over *you*. His joy will be your strength.

SECTION I

From
Grief
to Joy

FROM GRIEF TO JOY

Lord, you know all my desires and deepest longings. My tears are liquid words and you can read them all. My heart beats wildly, my strength is sapped, and the light of my eyes is going out.
—PSALM 38:9–11

FROM THE START OF HER LIFE, Annette felt her voice did not matter. The pain of molestation, and her molester's threats that she couldn't tell a soul, overshadowed the joy of carefree childhood days. Inner turmoil led her to the conclusion that she was unlovable, a person without worth. Because she didn't believe she could be loved for who she was, she detached from feeling love for herself or for others. Instead, Annette sought to earn love through performance. The truth of her identity was crushed.

As Annette grew older, the need to achieve significance continued to be a driving force in her life. If she could impress others, she would prove she was a lovable person, so she set her sights on becoming an architect. At nineteen years old, Annette was pursuing her dream and in a stable, happy relationship with her boyfriend—a relationship that could one day lead to marriage. Her boyfriend was thoughtful and kind, and he often brought roses to express his affection for her. When Annette learned she was pregnant, the future she envisioned was forever altered. She couldn't fathom how she'd be able to love her baby when she couldn't even love herself. Her emotions toward her baby were completely numb. Embarrassed and ashamed, she wanted to hide. She had been raised in a good Christian home but had turned away from her faith. If her parents found out about her pregnancy, it would demonstrate she was unworthy and unlovable, so she kept her secret hidden from them. She felt she had nowhere to turn. No one stood by her side to encourage her or tell her, "You can do this. I believe in you!"

Friends steered her to an abortion clinic, where the doctor and the nurses offered their counsel. "You should abort. That's the best decision for you." Naïve, scared, and vulnerable, Annette trusted their advice, as they seemed to know what they were talking about. But the clinic was unable to perform her abortion. An ultrasound revealed Annette was sixteen weeks pregnant, much farther along than she'd thought. "Your tissue is larger than allowed in Indiana," the technician told her bluntly. Annette felt the stinging chill of coldness emanate from this worker. It took her by surprise, and she wondered if the technician's job had contributed to the deadness of spirit that hardened her soul.

To have an abortion, Annette would have to cross state lines to Kentucky, where the abortion laws were more lenient. The following day, Annette's boyfriend drove her to Kentucky to an abortion clinic. He also felt pressure to live up to high moral standards set by his parents, but had fallen short. Out of desperation to hide his failure from them, he became complicit in the decision to end his baby's life.

Before she had her abortion, Annette didn't know what she was stepping into. However, the *moment* her abortion was complete, she had a spiritual awakening. "I knew I had taken the life of an innocent person," she recalled. When she experienced the drastic sting of death, her emotions roared to life, awakening her senses to feelings that had been buried. "For the first time I felt deep, deep sorrow for the loss of a person," Annette said. The weight of guilt and shame washed over her.

She could no longer look at babies or listen to their cries. These sights and sounds haunted her, and she ended the relationship with her boyfriend.

Giving in to abortion scarred Annette in more ways than she realized. She was terrified of becoming a mother. She was afraid she would hate her future children and abuse them. Because of her abortion, she felt she had partnered with the supreme child abuser, the devil. "Abortion is the worst form of child abuse there is," Annette said. "Because I partnered with him, I opened myself up to his voice in that area of abuse." The voice said she would be a bad mother—the voice that came from the father of lies.

Within a few years, Annette found herself pregnant again. This time she was married to a good man she loved, and it should have been the happiest time in her life—but she wasn't looking forward to bringing their child into the world. All her fears came flooding back. Yet the day she gave birth to their son, a miracle took place in Annette's heart. It was love at first sight. A new spiritual awakening overwhelmed her spirit—the revelation that she had bought into a dirty lie. She didn't hate her son. He didn't repulse her. The love she had for her newborn baby affected her profoundly. "This was the most amazing and joyful experience of my life," Annette said. In an instant, her mind understood a truth her spirit had known all along: *Abortion is wrong.* It wasn't just a piece of tissue that had been removed from her body. It was a baby.

Now the years following her abortion made sense. When she'd been feeling sad about her loss, her friends had deemed her baby insignificant and unlovable, invalidating Annette's feelings. They had told her, "You just had an abortion. There's nothing wrong with that." So she'd stuffed down her emotions, pretending the abortion hadn't bothered her. But in her spirit, she knew she had done something *really* wrong. She knew she had taken a life. With the permission to grieve denied, she'd had no place or space to mourn this loss of life. She'd *needed* to mourn her first baby's loss. It was the most natural thing to do. "And I couldn't," Annette said.

Grief over an abortion is rarely spoken aloud. Many who have aborted their children feel pressure to hide their emotions of grief and act like everything is okay. They don't realize that grief affects their entire being, whether they acknowledge their grief or hold it in. It is impossible to grieve and heal when you're worried about what other people think. Suppressing emotions is unhealthy, and to enter into healing and wholeness, you must be allowed to grieve.

Grief has a purpose. You wouldn't grieve if you didn't love.

After her son's birth, Annette continued to carry the heaviness of guilt and shame, unaware that the same antilife spirit behind abortion affected every area of her life. "One abuse leads to another," she said. Child abuse, self-abuse, and thoughts of suicide afflict many women who have experienced an abortion. Annette was distressed when she discovered that her own mothering instincts were compromised. Whispered lies continued to assault her mind—lies that said she would be a horrible mother, unable to love her son or feel connected to him. The temptation to agree with these lies was ever present, and she fought to preserve the truth.

Annette returned to the roots of her faith and started walking closely with the Lord. Then the pieces of her past fell into place, as she understood a spirit against humanity had attacked her identity from her youngest days, but those thoughts had not originated in her heart. The spirit was a liar. As she learned how to distinguish her own internal voice from the voice of her enemy, she would positively affirm the truth. "I am a good mother," she'd say. "I'm a *loving* mother. I love my child. I love him more than myself." With each affirmation, her mothering instincts were strengthened as the lies fell away. She continued to fight against this spirit by standing fast on the truth of God's word and wrapping herself in His love. During one of her times of worship and contemplation, Jesus gave her permission to mourn the loss of her first child. He promised to wipe her tears away. "That is when I received spiritual and soul healing," she said. "When I had permission to mourn, I sought Jesus for forgiveness. Then I had to forgive myself."

Annette shares wise counsel to anyone who is tormented by the trauma of abortion and needs to walk through mourning and forgiveness. She says, "Acknowledge there was a life, a purpose, and a destiny for your child. One of the most wonderful things you can do is give your child a name. Once you have named your child, acknowledge that God designed your child and that they were a person. God will then take you on a journey of forgiveness, love, and compassion you can't study for or know how to do on your own." Annette followed this advice herself. She asked the Lord to reveal to her the sex of her baby and named her daughter Rose to honor her child's birth father, even though he was no longer a part of her life. With her voice strengthened by love, Annette chose to bring value to Rose's life as she shared her testimony publicly, speaking out about her past and giving hope to others for their future.

The road of grief has provided Annette with insights she might never have known otherwise. "When your identity is suffering—and you don't love yourself—it's easy to throw another person's life away," she said. She is now acutely aware of the need each person has for understanding and valuing their own purpose in life, and offers these words of hope. "Life is precious. Your life has meaning," she says. "It's not because of what you do, but because of who you are. You were created highly valuable and highly loved." This is the truth of *your* identity—the truth that will set you free.

Joy

He has **TORN THE VEIL**
AND *lifted*
from me the sad
HEAVINESS of mourning.
He *wrapped*
me in the glory
garments of **GLADNESS.**

Psalm 30:11

DAY 1

In Times of Grief

My life's strength melts away with grief and sadness;
come strengthen me and encourage me with your words.
—Psalm 119:28

IN TIMES OF GRIEF, I surround you with My love.

My compassion reaches out and reaches in to touch those places left vulnerable and exposed. I will heal every wound of your soul.

PAUSE IN REFLECTION

Quiet your heart

It's easy to believe God loves others, but it might not be as easy to believe God truly loves you. You may believe in His love with your mind, even though you haven't experienced this truth in your heart.

Let your healing journey begin with this simple question: Jesus, why do You love me?

The Lord may give you a picture, or specific thoughts and impressions may come to mind. Record these thoughts now. Don't be afraid to receive. Open your heart and let His healing love flow.

PAUSE IN GOD'S PRESENCE

Listen for His voice

*Until now you've not been bold enough to ask the Father for a single
thing in my name, but now you can ask, and keep on asking him!
And you can be sure that you'll receive what you ask for,
and your joy will have no limits!*
—John 16:24

DAY 2

Grieving Loss

When Jesus looked at Mary and saw her weeping at his feet, and all her
friends who were with her grieving, he shuddered with emotion and
was deeply moved with tenderness and compassion.
—JOHN 11:33

THROUGH EVERY MOMENT OF YOUR LIFE, I have never
left you or abandoned you. My love for you goes deep and spreads wide.
I am with you now.

Hold onto My love in this time of grieving your loss. When others
fail you, remember that I never will. I am here for you—always.

PAUSE IN REFLECTION
Quiet your heart

Have you been denied permission to grieve? If so, open your heart as you bring your grief before the Lord. You can be real with God as you express your emotions honestly. He values this purity of your heart.

Ask Jesus to reveal Himself to you as you mourn the loss of your child. If you have not yet given your child a name, ask the Lord to help you. What do you hear Him saying to you?

PAUSE IN GOD'S PRESENCE

Listen for His voice

_____

_____

_____

_____

_____

_____

_____

_____

_____

_____

_____

_____

_____

_____

_____

_____

_____

_____

_____

_____

In mercy you have seen my troubles and you have cared for me;
even during this crisis in my soul I will be radiant with joy,
filled with praise for your love and mercy.
—PSALM 31:7

DAY 3

The Birthplace of Joy

And God raised us up with Christ and seated us with
him in the heavenly realms in Christ Jesus.
—Ephesians 2:6 niv

LIVE YOUR LIFE WITH THE QUIET CONFIDENCE that I am your God. I am for you, no matter what comes your way. When troubles do come, remember your place—you are seated with Me in the heavenly places, where My kingdom rules and reigns supreme over all.

In this place, no fear can penetrate. This is the birthplace of joy—joy that is your strength. This is the place for you. Come here often.

PAUSE IN REFLECTION
Quiet your heart

As you walk through these days of grieving the loss of your child, can you feel the presence of God draw near to you? In what ways does He make Himself known?

Write down these moments and hold onto them. These moments in His presence are given to strengthen your heart.

PAUSE IN GOD'S PRESENCE

Listen for His voice

_____

_____

_____

_____

_____

_____

_____

_____

_____

_____

_____

_____

_____

_____

_____

_____

_____

_____

*You will show me the path of life; in Your presence is fullness of joy;
at Your right hand are pleasures forevermore.*
—Psalm 16:11 NKJV

Joy Is Coming

Weeping may endure for a night, but joy comes in the morning.
—Psalm 30:5 NKJV

I AM NEAR TO THE BROKENHEARTED and I save those who are crushed in spirit. I am near to you.

The enemy has you in his sights because he knows your destiny is great. He is content to let you relax in your identity as long as you don't move forward into the destiny I have for you. But I say you will move confidently in both, as you are held firmly in My heart.

You are walking the path of suffering now, but joy is coming. Rest in My love and worship Me.

PAUSE IN REFLECTION

Quiet your heart

Grief is a journey filled with many opportunities for learning. Now is the time to focus on what God has redeemed.

What is your identity in Christ? Who does He say that you are? What are the plans He has purposed for your life? Do you believe the Lord can—and will—redeem and restore the destiny He has created for you?

PAUSE IN GOD'S PRESENCE

Listen for His voice

_____

_____

_____

_____

_____

_____

_____

_____

_____

_____

_____

_____

_____

_____

_____

_____

_____

_____

_____

Gaze upon him, join your life with his, and joy will come.
Your faces will glisten with glory.
You'll never wear that shame-face again.
—Psalm 34:5

Supernatural Joy

The humble also shall increase their joy in the LORD.
—ISAIAH 29:19 NKJV

FIND JOY IN ME. Make this a benchmark of your life. No matter what comes your way, take joy in the comfort of My love.

Joy is a supernatural gift from My heart because joy requires supernatural eyesight and sensitivity to see beyond the natural realm. It was for the joy set before Me that I endured the cross. I understand suffering, and I understand joy.

I impart My understanding and ability to you today. I will see you through.

PAUSE IN REFLECTION

Quiet your heart

Have you ever experienced this supernatural joy of the Lord? His joy tears down the strongholds of the enemy in your life. His joy is your weapon and your strength.

Ask the Lord to fill the empty places of your heart with His joy. Make it your choice to receive.

PAUSE IN GOD'S PRESENCE

Listen for His voice

_____
_____
_____
_____
_____
_____
_____
_____
_____
_____
_____
_____
_____
_____
_____
_____
_____
_____
_____
_____

Then my fears will dissolve into limitless joy;
my whole being will overflow with gladness
because of your mighty deliverance.
—Psalm 35:9

Just Be

"Before I formed you in the womb, I knew you,
and before you were born, I set you apart."
—JEREMIAH 1:5 TLV

IMAGINE THE MOMENT I conceived you in My heart. Picture your life in My womb, which is a place where all you needed flowed from Me. In this place you rested and grew in strength as you listened to the beat of My heart, surrounded by love and joy where you didn't need to perform—you just had to be.

My love always has been and always will be strong for you. I love you in completeness. I love you in joy. My heart is knitted to yours. You are constantly in My thoughts. I can do nothing less.

Rest in My love.

PAUSE IN REFLECTION

Quiet your heart

Do you believe God's love for you is tied to your performance? Do you believe that if you were a "better" person, God would love you more? Can you release the heaviness of these expectations back into His loving hands now?

Ask Jesus to touch your heart with the truth of His love.

PAUSE IN GOD'S PRESENCE

Listen for His voice

_____
_____
_____
_____
_____
_____
_____
_____
_____
_____
_____
_____
_____
_____
_____
_____
_____
_____
_____
_____

Let this hope burst forth within you, releasing a continual joy.
Don't give up in a time of trouble, but commune with
God at all times.
—ROMANS 12:12

DAY 7

The Desires of Your Heart

Give God the right to direct your life, and as you trust him along the way you'll find he pulled it off perfectly!
—Psalm 37:5

THE DESIRES YOU HOLD IN YOUR HEART are desires I planned for you before you were ever knitted together in your mother's womb. I am not in a hurry to see My plans unfold in your life, but I do wait for the intensity of your desire to ripen so that My plans may be fulfilled.

Activate the desires of your heart by praying as you ask, seek, and knock. Realize that for these dreams to come to life—dreams that I have planted—you must be willing to take action as I direct.

PAUSE IN REFLECTION

Quiet your heart

Have you abandoned the desires God placed in your heart? What has the enemy stolen that you need to reclaim? What does God want to release to you now?

If you're struggling to believe the Lord will restore your unfulfilled dreams and desires, make room in your heart for faith to rise up. Align your soul with His goodness.

PAUSE IN GOD'S PRESENCE

Listen for His voice

Now may God, the inspiration and fountain of hope, fill you to overflowing with uncontainable joy and perfect peace as you trust in Him.
—ROMANS 15:13

Follow My Call

You've gone into my future to prepare the way,
and in kindness you follow behind me to spare me from the harm of my past.
With your hand of love upon my life, you impart a blessing to me.
—PSALM 139:5

LISTEN TO ME. Keep your heart in ready obedience to follow My call in your life. With childlike faith like this, all things are possible.

You are able to conquer the mountains in your life because I am equipping you with everything you need. Those dreams that were once locked away and unattainable are now opened and within reach, because I hold a Yes! in My heart toward you.

Can you receive My goodness? Align your heart to believe in My promises for you.

PAUSE IN REFLECTION

Quiet your heart

Read Psalm 139:5 once more. Let these words penetrate into your soul and spirit. Open your ears to hear the Lord speak His blessing over your life.

Write down His words of love to you. What is one dream in your life He wants to fulfill?

PAUSE IN GOD'S PRESENCE

Listen for His voice

_____

_____

_____

_____

_____

_____

_____

_____

_____

_____

_____

_____

_____

_____

_____

_____

_____

_____

_____

_____

Let my passion for life be restored, tasting joy in every breakthrough you bring to me. Hold me close to you with a willing spirit that obeys whatever you say.
—PSALM 51:12

SECTION II

From
Guilt to
Forgiveness

I'm overwhelmed, swamped, and submerged beneath the heavy burden
of my guilt. It clings to me and won't let me go.
—Psalm 38:4

THE WORLD SANK ITS CLAWS DEEP into Michael's life. His
mother was a strong believer who'd taught him about Jesus, and when
he was fourteen years old, his dad was radically saved and transformed.
Although Michael was raised in a home that had a firm grasp of God's
heart, his eyes were veiled to the truth of God's love. Living in the
world—and living for self—appealed to him more than living for the
Lord. He hadn't yet encountered the beauty of God's presence. "I had
no clue of the goodness of God," Michael said. "I had no clue He was
full of joy." He didn't understand how deeply God longed to make
Himself known.

By the time he was nineteen, Michael was heavily involved in
drugs, perversion, and rebellion. "I was a hedonist," Michael said. "I
was a pleasure seeker." He sought pleasure in all the wrong places. Sin
is only fun for a period of time, and he was out to grab all the fun he
could get. As his addictions intensified, his life spiraled out of control.
While drunk one night, Michael took his dad's truck out for a spin,
speeding recklessly in the dark on a treacherous one-lane road. His tires

lost traction on the wet surface of the road, causing the truck to careen into another vehicle and a few trees before coming to a stop. The truck was crushed, but Michael walked away unscathed. Police arrived on the scene and found a stash of drugs he'd thrown from the window to evade detection of drug possession. Michael was placed in handcuffs and taken to jail as his mother watched in tears.

During this downward spiral, he sought to ease the emptiness of his heart by chasing girls, and he engaged in one relationship after another. After an immoral relationship with one girlfriend who could not fill the void in his life, they broke up. Several weeks later, she returned with news he dreaded. She was pregnant and certain he was the father. After discussing the situation with her mother, they decided an abortion was the best solution—and they wanted *him* to pay for the procedure. Michael was stunned. He loved kids, and he had an innate desire to be a father. He had a good job that paid well. And yet he knew he was irresponsible. He didn't think he could handle the responsibility of parenthood at that time in his life—it was too soon. He bought into this lie from the enemy—hook, line, and sinker. Michael gave her the money for the abortion and kept this secret locked in his heart, repressing his emotions deep within.

Unresolved guilt can fuel anxiety, leading to physical symptoms of headaches, stomachaches, muscle tension, and sleeplessness. Emotional disturbances can surface, causing desperation, defensiveness, irritability, and sorrow. For Michael, depression rushed in like a flood. Nothing could satisfy him or make him happy, and thoughts of suicide plagued his mind. His parents noticed his despondency and pressed in to pray. When he couldn't bear the shame and regret of his decision any longer, Michael turned to God for relief. In his room he found his Bible, layered with dust. He opened it, and the Word came alive to his spirit. Michael got real with God. "I need You," he cried. "Change me. Have Your way in my life—whatever You need to do."

Immediately the love of God consumed his heart. He heard the inner voice of the Holy Spirit speak to him. *Son! Son, I have plans for your life.* Michael experienced the tangible glory of God. "His glory is our inheritance. Anything else is a rip-off," he explained. Once he tasted the pleasure of God, his emptiness was filled. He broke away from the addiction to drugs. His journey to healing had begun.

One Sunday, Michael's sister invited him to come with her to the megachurch in their area. He reluctantly agreed to go, as he wasn't interested in church. Before he left, he made a bargain with God. "Lord, I have so many burdens weighing me down," he said. "If You kindly remove one of them in church today, I promise I'll come to church from now on." He sat through the two-hour service, unimpressed. Where was the answer to his prayer? Why was God silent? When the pastor gave the altar call, Michael stormed out of the sanctuary. He could still hear the pastor's voice as the audio from the service streamed into the restroom. The pastor released a word of knowledge. "Someone in here is suffering with shame from going through an abortion," the pastor said. "Come to the altar, and God will heal your heart." Michael knew it was a word from God to him.

He ran out of the restroom, trying desperately to find his way back into the sanctuary to respond to the pastor's invitation. Each set of doors he tried to open were locked. He returned to the restroom and locked himself in a stall. "God will meet you in the most unusual places. I opened up my heart to Him and felt His love pour into me," Michael said. There was no condemnation. God's glorious forgiveness and love removed his guilt, shame, and pain. He experienced the Father's embrace. Michael left that restroom stall a changed man, completely free from shame.

Several months later, he was in church again. This time it was Father's Day. When the pastor invited the fathers in the room to stand, Michael remained in his seat. *I'm not a dad*, he thought. Then he heard the Lord speak to his heart. *Son, Happy Father's Day*. Tears streamed down his face as a fresh wave of healing washed over his heart. Not only was he forgiven, but now he realized he had a child in heaven he would see one day—a reunion where there would be no animosity or hatred, just pure love. This new layer of revelation ministered deeply to his soul.

A few years later, Michael traveled to Mozambique, Africa, to serve as a missionary. In a time of worship and prayer, the Lord gave him a vision of heaven. He saw Jesus walking toward him, holding a baby. He placed the baby in Michael's arms. Then Jesus spoke. *This is your baby. He's a son. And his name is Stephen.* Michael's heart melted with joy. His child was a son who had a name!

Michael met his wife, Selina, in Mozambique, where they ministered to the poor. Today they are the proud parents of two beautiful children and are the founders of Life Poured Out International, a ministry with a vision to reach the lost, ignite the church, and serve the poor.

Michael has an unrelenting passion to spread the good news of Christ to the nations—good news that includes the forgiveness only Christ can give. Because he experienced the power of forgiveness that brought freedom from his guilt and shame of abortion, he wants those who are suffering to know the hope God imparts to wounded hearts. Michael says, "You may think you're unforgiveable and wonder, *How can God forgive me for what I've done? Abortion is murder.* But the Lord lovingly forgave me. Let the Lord touch you right now. He'll do it, just like He did it for me."

There is healing in the presence of the Lord.

Michael has this prayer for you to pray in faith as you invite the Lord to heal the hurts of your heart:

Holy Spirit, I know I've sinned against You. But I also know that where sin abounds, grace abounds all the more. Thank You for your never-ending mercy. I open my heart to You. Remove all pain and shame. Erase regret and guilt from my life. Fill my heart with Your peace and comfort. I know my child is with you in heaven and we'll be united together there. May I walk in Your hope and freedom from this day forward. I forgive myself for the mistakes I've made. I forgive those who have sinned against me. Now let this be a testimony for Your glory! Amen.

Forgiveness

YOU
kissed
my **HEART** with
forgiveness
in spite of
all I've **DONE.**

 PSALM 103:3

Refining Fire

*Lord, you can scrutinize me. Refine my heart and probe my every
thought. Put me to the test and you'll find it's true.*
—PSALM 26:2

KEEP YOUR HEART HUMBLE and soft before Me. I expose areas
that are hidden from your sight, so you may grow in My grace and mercy
as I conform you to My image. The closer you draw to Me, the more I
will expose. This is a good thing! Would you rather continue with your
eyes blinded to your own sin, living for self and apart from My glory?

Draw near to My refining fire. The dross will rise to surface so it
may be removed—and what is left is pure gold.

PAUSE IN REFLECTION

Quiet your heart

Are you willing to draw near to the Lord's refining fire, or does fear keep you away? What is God showing you about His character and nature in this time of cleansing?

Let His love draw you close.

PAUSE IN GOD'S PRESENCE

Listen for His voice

_____
_____
_____
_____
_____
_____
_____
_____
_____
_____
_____
_____
_____
_____
_____
_____
_____
_____
_____
_____

Without this revelation-light, how would I ever detect the waywardness of my heart? Lord, forgive my hidden flaws whenever you find them.
—Psalm 19:12

Embrace My Correction

Fully embrace God's correction as part of your training, for he is doing
what any loving father does for his children. For who has ever heard of
a child who never had to be corrected?
—Hebrews 12:7

KEEP YOUR HEART CLEAN before Me at all times. You do this as you stay sensitive to My Holy Spirit. Do not block the flow of His communication with you because you are afraid of what He might uncover.

Openness to correction from My Holy Spirit brings life and wisdom to you. Correction is only effective if you partner with My words to create avenues for change in your attitudes and behavior. Confession with repentance is the first step to releasing My life flow.

Embrace correction. Know that this is My desire for your good, as you are conformed to My image.

PAUSE IN REFLECTION
Quiet your heart

Is it difficult for you to receive correction? As a child, how did you experience correction from your father? Did he learn how to correct in love, or was he harsh and abusive?

If trauma from correction lingers, invite the Holy Spirit to draw near to you now so He may begin to heal this hurt of your heart.

PAUSE IN GOD'S PRESENCE

Listen for His voice

_____

_____

_____

_____

_____

_____

_____

_____

_____

_____

_____

_____

_____

_____

_____

_____

_____

_____

_____

Many are the sorrows and frustrations of those who don't come clean with God. But when you trust in the Lord for forgiveness, his wrap-around love will surround you.
—Psalm 32:10

No Excuses

My child, when the Lord God speaks to you, never take his words lightly, and never be upset when he corrects you. For the Father's discipline comes only from his passionate love and pleasure for you.
—Proverbs 3:11–12

DON'T MAKE EXCUSES for sin. If My Holy Spirit starts to bring conviction, rebuke, or correction, do not minimize His work. Instead, partner with Him and listen, and then obey. Keep your heart sensitized to Me, whether it is convenient or not, whether it is easy or not. This is how you remain in the blessing of My covenant and favor.

Are you willing to listen to Me?

PAUSE IN REFLECTION

Quiet your heart

When is the last time you made an excuse for sin? Are you making excuses now? The kindness of God leads to repentance (see Romans 2:4). Are you afraid to hear God's voice speak to you regarding sin?

Remember, there is no fear in love. Receive His forgiveness. Listen as love speaks to your heart.

PAUSE IN GOD'S PRESENCE

Listen for His voice

---

*Always look at me through your eyes of love—your forgiving
eyes of mercy and compassion.*
—Psalm 25:16

My Truth Reveals

So Lord, don't hold back your love or withhold your tender mercies
from me. Keep me in your truth and let your compassion overflow to me
no matter what I face.
—Psalm 40:11

I REVEAL TRUTH not to hurt hearts but to heal.

My truth is always accompanied with an invitation to come up higher, to step into greater revelation and understanding. The choice is yours.

How will you respond to truth? Will anger and defensiveness consume you so that you turn away, or will humility and repentance lead you closer to My heart?

My truth reveals the secrets locked in your heart of hearts.

PAUSE IN REFLECTION

Quiet your heart

What do these words reveal about your heart? Are there secrets you've locked away that the Lord wants to reveal?

Allow the Lord to minister to these hidden places as you open your heart to Him.

PAUSE IN GOD'S PRESENCE

Listen for His voice

*Lord, if you measured us and marked us with our sins, who would ever
have their prayers answered? But your forgiving love is what makes you so
wonderful. No wonder you are loved and worshiped!*
—PSALM 130:3–4

The Healer of Hearts

Wait on the LORD; be of good courage, and He shall strengthen your heart.
—PSALM 27:14 NKJV

I AM THE HEALER of hearts. I am healing your heart from the wounds of hurts and insults so that you can love with greater abandon.

You do not need to fear love's hurts. When you turn your heart to follow Me in those times, you open the channel for greater levels of love to be increased, and your foundation of love grows stronger still.

Shore up the foundation of your heart by choosing My ways over your own. Choose wisely.

PAUSE IN REFLECTION

Quiet your heart

Do you believe Jesus is the Healer of your heart? Is it difficult to accept He cares about every facet of your life, especially those areas that continue to cause you pain? What truth do you find in His word that confirms His love for you?

Ask Him for a verse of promise that magnifies His heart of compassion over your life.

PAUSE IN GOD'S PRESENCE

Listen for His voice

_____
_____
_____
_____
_____
_____
_____
_____
_____
_____
_____
_____
_____
_____
_____
_____
_____
_____
_____

Our hero, come and rescue us!
O God of the breakthrough, for the glory of your name, come
and help us! Forgive and restore us; heal us and cover us in your love.
—PSALM 79:9

Mature Love

Those who are loved by God, let his love continually
pour from you to one another, because God is love.
—1 JOHN 4:7

THE MORE DEEPLY YOU LOVE, the more opportunities there are for your heart to be hurt by the unkindness, the insults, and the cruelties of others. How you respond in these situations demonstrates the level of maturity in the love you hold.

Mature love rises above insult to demonstrate My heart that I impart to you. Do not think that in these times you need to rely on your own strength. Rely on My strength. Ask to see as I see. Ask to love as I love.

I will impart supernatural strength into your heart for you to move past the offense, allowing you to forgive.

PAUSE IN REFLECTION
Quiet your heart

How are you doing in the area of forgiveness? What is your greatest challenge in this area? Have you been able to receive God's forgiveness? If so, do you forgive others as you have been forgiven, or do offenses keep you bound?

Ask the Lord to show you His solution to your need.

PAUSE IN GOD'S PRESENCE
Listen for His voice

_____
_____
_____
_____
_____
_____
_____
_____
_____
_____
_____
_____
_____
_____
_____
_____
_____
_____
_____
_____

But instead be kind and affectionate toward one another. Has God graciously forgiven you? Then graciously forgive one another in the depths of Christ's love.
—Ephesians 4:32

Choose Love

I continue to pray for your love to grow and increase beyond measure,
bringing you into the rich revelation of spiritual insight in all things.
—Philippians 1:9

I CALL YOU TO FORGIVE AS I FORGIVE. I call you to love as I love. These actions are not easy, and they come at a price. But they are necessary if you want to become more like Me.

As you walk in obedience and faith, more of My love will be imparted to you. You will grow in favor and discernment, releasing My wisdom into every situation where you have a need. Which is more preferable? To walk in love or to walk as you wish? The trade-off is clear.

Choose love.

PAUSE IN REFLECTION

Quiet your heart

How are you doing in the area of love? What does love look like to you? How does love behave? Love is a demonstration, not an inclination of the heart. Love moves into action.

What actions do you need to take today to demonstrate love to God and love to others?

PAUSE IN GOD'S PRESENCE

Listen for His voice

---

*Therefore I tell you, her sins, which are many,
are forgiven—for she loved much.*
—LUKE 7:47 ESV

DAY 16

Freedom for Your Soul

Lay aside bitter words, temper tantrums, revenge, profanity,
and insults. But instead be kind and affectionate toward one another.
Has God graciously forgiven you? Then graciously forgive
one another in the depths of Christ's love.
—Ephesians 4:31–32

DO NOT LET BITTERNESS CREEP INTO YOUR HEART. Is it possible to say you have forgiven while you allow festering bitterness to remain? Forgive fully by releasing all bitterness and anger. Move in the opposite spirit. Walk in joy, which is freedom for your soul.

This is how you defeat the purposes of the enemy in your situation. Love from the depths of My resources which never run out. You can do it!

PAUSE IN REFLECTION
Quiet your heart

Bitterness can keep you chained in a prison of unforgiveness. Offenses, no matter how large or small, cannot remain if you want to walk in freedom.

Read Psalm 139:23–24 out loud. Ask the Lord to search your heart and uncover any lingering bitterness. Release every offense to Him. Receive His love for the ones who have hurt you. Are you ready to be set free?

PAUSE IN GOD'S PRESENCE

Listen for His voice

O Israel, keep hoping, keep trusting, and keep waiting on the Lord,
for he is tenderhearted, kind, and forgiving.
He has a thousand ways to set you free!
—Psalm 130:7

From
Shame
to Grace

I confess all my sin to you; I can't hold it in any longer.
My agonizing thoughts punish me for my wrongdoing;
I feel condemned as I consider all I've done.
—PSALM 38:18

KAY LYN KNEW if she ever became pregnant before she was ready to have a child, abortion would be her option of choice. Representatives from the local women's clinic had prepared her heart when they entered her grade school to teach the students about sex education and abortion.

Growing up, Kay Lyn tried to live a perfect life, but she had no joy. She felt like she was a constant disappointment to God. Though she accepted Jesus when she was a young child, she learned from her dad the ways of legalism. God was an angry God, and she was a filthy rag in His sight. "Every sin has a consequence," her dad would say. "It will be like a dark cloud looming over you the rest of your life."

In high school, she rebelled by dating a boy she knew her parents didn't like, though she knew if she ever got pregnant, her dad would kick her out of the house and cut off all help. She was a cheerleader, both popular and conceited. Her classmates judged girls who got pregnant and kept their babies, referring to them as "sluts." Though she felt sympathy for their situations, Kay Lyn didn't want to be known by that label. "I didn't think it could happen to me," she said. Only it could. And it did.

Kay Lyn stood in a phone booth with her boyfriend and dialed the clinic. A voice on the other end said, "Congratulations, you're pregnant!" Overwhelmed by the startling news, she let out an uncontrollable scream that embodied her shock, crisis, and emotional pain. Her boyfriend tried to console her, but it was no use. She turned on him in blame. *He* should have been more careful. Kay Lyn had no desire to marry her boyfriend at just seventeen years old. She had been using him and quickly rejected his offer of marriage. She didn't waste any time in scheduling her abortion.

In the clinic waiting room, an upset Kay Lyn rocked back and forth in her chair, which made the other girls nervous. An attendant offered her the opportunity to speak with a counselor, but she declined because she thought the counselor would try to talk her out of getting an abortion. Her resolve only grew stronger. Kay Lyn asked a worker if the life growing inside of her was a baby. "No," the worker said, "it's a clump of tissue, a cluster of cells. It's a product of conception." This brought her a measure of peace and the permission she needed to proceed.

During the abortion, her body shook uncontrollably. Her parents didn't know she was pregnant, and she had crossed the state line so they wouldn't find out. As she disassociated from her situation, visions of herself filled her mind—a little girl being held in her mother's arms, safe and secure. Abruptly, she brought her thoughts back. *No! You can't go there.* Kay Lyn was farther along in her pregnancy than she'd realized. Her abortion took much longer than expected and was excruciatingly painful. She was afraid. "How much longer will this take?" she asked.

An attendant answered reassuringly. "Remember, dear, once the vacuum turns on, it's only going to take twenty seconds longer. You can go home and never have to think about it again. Your parents will never have to know. You can get on with your life, and everything will be put back to normal."

As the doctor pulled the instruments out of her body, a warm stream ran down her legs. The sensation was comforting until she noticed it was blood. *There's been blood shed today*, she thought. The reality hit her hard. "Was it a boy or girl?" Kay Lyn asked. She wanted to know.

The once-nice workers turned stone cold. "What does it matter now?" an attendant responded.

She resolved never to think of her abortion again. She would go on and live her life. However, her boyfriend was a constant reminder of what she had done. A short time after the abortion, she broke up with him. Kay Lyn graduated from high school and entered into a new relationship. She married quickly to run away from her problems, expecting her husband to fix everything. Even though she was married, she never wanted to become a mother. "I didn't have that mother gene," she said.

Seven years into her marriage, she heard familiar words that struck fear in her heart. "Congratulations, you're pregnant!" Her first thought was to abort her child. She asked her husband if he wanted her to get an abortion. He didn't hesitate. "No. I think we can do this." That simple word of encouragement held the difference between life and death for her growing baby. The next day her husband brought home a gift—a baby bib with the words "I ♥ Mommy." For the first time, Kay Lyn opened the door of her heart to come to terms with her abortion. This little bib personalized the connection she had with her first baby, bringing her child's memory to a conscious level in her mind.

When Kay Lyn went in for her first ultrasound, she saw her growing baby on the monitor. She could make out the different parts of her little body. "Oh look, your baby's waving at you!" the ultrasound technician said. Kay Lyn was traumatized. This baby was two weeks *younger* than the baby she had aborted, and she snapped out of her cloud of denial. She realized she had betrayed innocent blood. *Look at what you've done!* Tears coursed down her face. She felt an overwhelming urge to bolt from the table. "I wanted to run . . . to run away from myself," she said. Seized with remorse, Kay Lyn didn't know how God could want to have anything to do with her.

Kay Lyn gave birth to her daughter Emily prematurely, a risk factor common for mothers who have undergone abortion. Graphic nightmares tormented her sleep, vivid pictures that Emily's life was in peril. She was afraid she was going to destroy her baby girl. Attachment issues persisted, so her husband stepped in to care for Emily while Kay Lyn learned how to bond with her baby.

Kay Lyn was not alone. Many post-abortive women also face attachment issues with future children. She loved God, but she struggled with her identity. Psalm 139 did not bring her comfort. When she read the words "I am fearfully and wonderfully made," she could only think of herself as a murderer of the child who had been in her womb. Everyone was invited into the kingdom of God—everyone except for her. She had committed an unforgiveable sin.

For years, anxiety and depression consumed her thoughts. She believed her destiny was to live a shame-filled life, which filled her with hopelessness. Though she and her husband were strongly involved in their church, on the leadership team, and successful leaders of the youth, Kay Lyn felt she was leading a fake life. "God, open up the floor and take me to hell," she prayed. She already felt she was living in hell on earth. Haunted by her past, she wanted to die.

Research shows that post-abortive women have a higher likelihood of committing suicide than women who carry their babies full term. Depression, anxiety, post-traumatic stress disorder (PTSD) symptoms, and suicide ideation afflict many post-abortive women and men. Her abortion was the root of her anxiety and depression. She sought help from her pastor, who affirmed her identity and validated her as a dear Christian friend. He showed her John 3:17: "God did not send his Son into the world to condemn the world, but to save the world through him." Her heart melted. This was so different from what she had been taught as a child. The pastor said she was struggling in the area of faith and needed to believe God at His word. "You need to go get yourself some faith," he said. This revelation opened the door for Kay Lyn's healing journey to begin.

It was time to make amends with others. Kay Lyn made an appointment to meet with her parents, who didn't know she'd had an abortion. Shame had kept her from telling them the truth. She faced her parents and told them she was sorry. Kay Lyn's dad was the first to respond. "There's nothing you can do that would separate my love from you. You're forgiven, Kay Lyn," he said.

She raised her eyes to meet her mom's gaze. "Kay Lyn, how can we help you with this?" her mom asked. These were not the responses she'd expected. This was a spiritual experience for her.

The heavens opened up and God came down. He said, *Kay Lyn, your earthly parents can love you this much. How much more is My love for you?* Kay Lyn couldn't fathom how much God loved her, but she could feel it. His love was wonderful. Step by step, God led her on her journey of healing as she walked in obedience to Him. Still, a cloud of shame covered her mind and heart, and she wondered if the dark cloud was from God. But in her heart, questions formed whether this was truly His voice or not.

One morning Kay Lyn heard her son, Ethan, playing in the living room. He was rolling around on the coffee table, having a good time. Abruptly, his play ended, and he cried, "Mom . . . Mom . . . Oh my gosh, Mom! I've ruined it. Oh my gosh, I've ruined it!" Ethan ran to her. "I've ruined the coffee table! You have to come see it!" He was distraught.

Kay Lyn wasn't concerned about the table. It was a twenty-five-dollar find at a garage sale. Whatever had happened was easy to forgive. But

Ethan wouldn't accept her words of forgiveness. She had to come see his transgression for herself. She followed him to examine the damage of only a few scratches on the table. "It's okay, Ethan. You're forgiven."

With his face red and flushed from crying, Ethan said, "Mom! You can't forgive me for *this* one." A panicked expression crossed his face. "Oh my gosh. You're going to have to tell Dad!"

"Ethan! You're forgiven. It's okay." All she wanted was to forget about the incident and have Ethan return to his normal, happy self. But he continued to cry. In exasperation, she said, "Ethan, my grace is sufficient for you!"

The heavens opened up again, and God spoke clearly to her heart. *Kay Lyn, your earthly grace for your son is sufficient for him. How much more, My dear child, is My grace sufficient for you? You have two choices. You can choose My grace, which is sufficient for you, or you can live a life of shame and despair. It's up to you.*

Like Ethan, who thought his transgression was too big for her to forgive, she had held on to her sin of abortion as too big for God to forgive. His grace was sufficient for *this* one. Kay Lyn chose His grace, and her shame was gone.

Today Kay Lyn is a professional counselor and therapist who helps those who have suffered from the devastation of abortion. She is the founder and director of Choose Grace International. She is still married to the husband of her youth, and together they have three beautiful children.

Abortion had nearly killed her—but God's grace made her whole.

Grace

So here's what I've **learned** THROUGH IT ALL: **LEAVE** all your cares and **ANXIETIES** at the feet of the **Lord**, AND measureless grace will **STRENGTHEN** you.

PSALM 55:22

The Gift of Grace

So now we come freely and boldly to where love is enthroned,
to receive mercy's kiss and discover the grace we urgently need
to strengthen us in our time of weakness.
—Hebrews 4:16

MY GRACE IS SUFFICIENT FOR YOU.

My grace carries you and covers the hurts of your heart. My grace renews and refreshes, bringing life out of death as it restores hope to the living.

My grace is a gift—an unearned treasure I pour out on those I love. I pour out My grace on you. You are loved far more than you could ever imagine.

Open your eyes to see.

PAUSE IN REFLECTION

Quiet your heart

Are you able to discern the grace of God in your life? Read 2 Corinthians 12:7–10. Through his weakness, Paul discovered grace, the empowering presence of God giving him strength. Your weakness gives opportunity for God's grace to empower you, helping you to overcome the challenges you face.

Identify the areas where you need grace to grow. Invite His empowering presence to conquer your fears.

PAUSE IN GOD'S PRESENCE
Listen for His voice

_____

_____

_____

_____

_____

_____

_____

_____

_____

_____

_____

_____

_____

_____

_____

_____

_____

_____

_____

_____

But he said to me, "My grace is sufficient for you, for my power is made perfect in weakness." Therefore I will boast all the more gladly of my weaknesses, so that the power of Christ may rest upon me.
—2 CORINTHIANS 12:9 ESV

I See You

My dearest one, let me tell you how I see you.
—Song of Songs 1:9

I CONTINUE TO EXPAND your vision so that you can see yourself with the eyes of My heart. I see you with longing, I see you with delight. One by one, I am removing the bricks of the wall that separates you from fully experiencing the love I have for you.

Open your understanding to experience My love. Open your heart to receive My love. Receive, so that you may be filled to all fullness as My life pours out in you.

Receive, so you may give.

PAUSE IN REFLECTION

Quiet your heart

What is your understanding of God? How do you see Him? Is He an angry God or a loving Father?

If your heart feels distant from God because of your past—or even your present—ask Him this question: "How do you see me?" Write down the impressions He places on your heart. He will answer you.

PAUSE IN GOD'S PRESENCE

Listen for His voice

_____

_____

_____

_____

_____

_____

_____

_____

_____

_____

_____

_____

_____

_____

_____

_____

_____

_____

_____

*God called me by his grace; and in love,
he chose me from my birth to be his.*
—GALATIANS 1:15

Move Closer

The steps of the God-pursuing ones follow firmly in the footsteps of the
Lord, and God delights in every step they take to follow him.
—Psalm 37:23

I VALUE THE TIME YOU SET BEFORE ME, even if it's not perfect in your eyes. Your desire is what matters most to Me, and your willingness to be obedient, even if it is hard.

Keep moving your heart closer and closer to Me as I move My heart closer and closer to you until no empty space in your heart remains. I fill you with the fullness of all that I am. I pour My life into you. I delight in you.

Let these words penetrate your heart, sinking in to the depths of your soul.

PAUSE IN REFLECTION
Quiet your heart

What is your "closeness quotient" to God? Is it easy to come near to His presence, or do you prefer to approach Him cautiously from a distance? Closeness, communication, and commitment are vital to growing in intimacy with Him.

What is one step you can take today to move closer to the Lord?

PAUSE IN GOD'S PRESENCE

Listen for His voice

*But continue to grow and increase in God's grace and intimacy with
our Lord and Savior, Jesus Christ. May he receive all the glory both
now and until the day eternity begins. Amen.*
—2 PETER 3:18

Inward Transformation

Stop imitating the ideals and opinions of the culture around you, but be inwardly transformed by the Holy Spirit through a total reformation of how you think. This will empower you to discern God's will as you live a beautiful life, satisfying and perfect in his eyes.
—ROMANS 12:2

THE MORE TIME YOU CHOOSE to spend in My presence, the more you become like Me—taking on My nature, being transformed to My image by the renewing of your mind. This is how the fruit of My Spirit grows and expands in your life.

As you submit yourself to these practices, you allow your spirit to reign over your mind and body. Grow strong in Me.

PAUSE IN REFLECTION

Quiet your heart

Does the process of inner transformation seem overwhelming? Have you tried to change negative attitudes but continue to fall back into your old patterns of thinking? If you are a believer in Jesus, the same Spirit that raised Him from the dead now lives in you (see Romans 8:11). That's powerful!

Call on His name to help you with the transformation you need. Focus on one aspect of His character that you'd like to emulate in your life. Worship Him now.

PAUSE IN GOD'S PRESENCE

Listen for His voice

_____

_____

_____

_____

_____

_____

_____

_____

_____

_____

_____

_____

_____

_____

_____

_____

_____

_____

_____

*This superabundant grace is already powerfully working in us,
releasing within us all forms of wisdom and
practical understanding.*
—Ephesians 1:8

In the Face of Adversity

Lord, strengthen my inner being by the promises of your word
so that I may live faithful and unashamed for you.
—PSALM 119:116

IN THE FACE OF ADVERSITY, press in for My promises. Lay hold of Me and do not let go.

Set your eyesight higher, above what you see in the natural realm. Because you believe in My superior truth, you anger the demonic realm. The enemy cannot make inroads against your faith without your cooperation.

Hold fast. Fight on.

PAUSE IN REFLECTION

Quiet your heart

Does shame harass you and remind you of your past? Fight your enemy of shame with promises from His word. Read Psalm 3:3 out loud: "But in the depths of my heart I truly know that you, Yahweh, have become my Shield; you take me and surround me with yourself. Your glory covers me continually. You lift high my head when I bow low in shame."

Command shame to leave. Allow His grace to fill every broken place in your heart.

PAUSE IN GOD'S PRESENCE

Listen for His voice

_____
_____
_____
_____
_____
_____
_____
_____
_____
_____
_____
_____
_____
_____
_____
_____
_____
_____

So then, prepare your hearts and minds for action!
Stay alert and fix your hope firmly on the marvelous grace
that is coming to you. For when Jesus Christ is unveiled,
a greater measure of grace will be released to you.
—1 PETER 1:13

The Heart of Faith

We look away from the natural realm and we fasten our gaze onto Jesus
who birthed faith within us and who leads us forward
into faith's perfection.
—Hebrews 12:2

I AM DEVELOPING GREAT FAITH IN YOU. When you face the trials of life, how do you respond?

Agreement with Me is the heart of faith. Agreement looks to My spiritual truth above the natural realities you see in this world. Agreement centers your heart during the storms of life and is the anchor that fastens your heart to Mine.

Take courage in My words of life over you.

PAUSE IN REFLECTION

Quiet your heart

Encourage your heart with 1 Corinthians 1:4–9. Can you receive this word of God as a word for you? It takes faith to agree with God over the natural circumstances in your life.

In what circumstance do you need faith to grow? Trust Him with that part of your heart. Agree that He is good. Agree that He is forever faithful and worthy of your trust.

PAUSE IN GOD'S PRESENCE

Listen for His voice

*I am always thanking God for you because he has given you such free
and open access to his grace through your union with Jesus, the Messiah.*
—1 CORINTHIANS 1:4

DAY 23

Hold Fast

Only hold fast what you have until I come.
—Revelation 2:25 esv

IT IS ONLY THROUGH FAITH that you can choose Me. I am the author and perfecter of your faith. Every day that you come with intention of heart to hear from Me, you activate your faith and it grows stronger.

Consider what this looks like in the heavenly realm. Your faith is beautiful to Me! It is a container of My life that continuously expands and is filled. This process is repeated every time you choose Me. It is an unending circle of delight that will never be broken as you hold fast to Me.

PAUSE IN REFLECTION

Quiet your heart

Is it your joy to enter into the presence of God? Or do you see this as a chore, one more thing to check off on your "to-do" list? Even the smallest step forward will reap a huge reward because it is the step of childlike faith.

Return to that place of wonder and find rest in that place of joy.

PAUSE IN GOD'S PRESENCE

Listen for His voice

_____
_____
_____
_____
_____
_____
_____
_____
_____
_____
_____
_____
_____
_____
_____
_____
_____
_____
_____

*And then, after your brief suffering, the God of all loving grace, who
has called you to share in his eternal glory in Christ, will personally
and powerfully restore you and make you stronger than ever.
Yes, he will set you firmly in place and build you up.*
—1 PETER 5:10

Faith Shines

Your faith and love rise within you as you access all the treasures
of your inheritance stored up in the heavenly realm.
—Colossians 1:5

FAITH ATTRACTS REWARD. Great reward awaits those who step out in great faith.

Faith encounters obstacles and pushes us through. Faith decimates objections. Faith calls on the host of heaven to defeat opposition.

In the eyes of the world, faith looks foolish. In the eyes of heaven, faith shines like gold.

Choose faith.

PAUSE IN REFLECTION

Quiet your heart

What is one step of faith that calls to you now? Do you need more faith to believe God has forgiven your sin and removed your shame? Do you need more faith to receive His love for you? Or do you face an impossible situation that only He can help?

Access the treasures of your inheritance stored up for you in the heavenly realm. Let your faith shine!

PAUSE IN GOD'S PRESENCE

Listen for His voice

_____

_____

_____

_____

_____

_____

_____

_____

_____

_____

_____

_____

_____

_____

_____

_____

_____

_____

_____

Since we are now joined to Christ, we have been given the treasures of redemption by his blood—the total cancellation of our sins—all because of the cascading riches of his grace.
—Ephesians 1:7

SECTION IV

From

Regret to
Comfort

I am completely broken because of what I've done. Gloom is all around me.
My sins have bent me over to the ground.
—Psalm 38:6

UNMARRIED, PREGNANT, AND AFRAID, Tegra felt trapped when she first stepped into an abortion clinic as a nineteen-year-old college student. Fear had led her to their doors. She called herself a Christian—but she had one foot in the church and one foot in the world. She'd asked her mother to take her to the clinic, and her mother agreed. "I believed it was just a blob of tissue. I had to believe a lie in order to do such an act," Tegra explained. A spirit of deception had fooled them both.

A worker took Tegra into the examination room, where an ultrasound was performed to determine the gestational age of the baby. Curious, she asked to see the monitor. Suddenly all niceties were pushed aside. "No! We don't do that here," the worker said.

"I do believe God provides a way of escape. It was in that moment I should have put my clothes on and run out," Tegra said. "I failed to act." She stayed and had the abortion. The first feeling of regret came the moment she left the clinic. Tegra and her mother drove home in silence. She never wanted to think about her abortion again, and she moved on with her life. Years would pass before she'd be able to talk with her mom about her experience that day. Tegra returned to college, graduated, and began her career, moving through her checklist of accomplishments to appear successful while masking the hole left in her heart.

Ten years after her abortion, Tegra married Marc, a wonderful man who loved God and became a pastor in their church. He didn't know anything about her abortion history, and she saw no reason to tell him. They both wanted to start a family right away, but their road to parenthood was filled with frustration, broken dreams, and sorrow. Five years into their marriage, Tegra became pregnant. She was diagnosed with an ectopic molar pregnancy, a rare occurrence that requires surgery and is treated as a fertility-related cancer. Two years later, Tegra became pregnant with their second child, which she lost to miscarriage. Still they did not give up on their hopes of becoming parents. Another year passed before she became pregnant with their third child. But she would not give birth to this baby either. Instead, she needed a partial hysterectomy due to another molar pregnancy. The dreams of having a baby were gone. She would not be able to bear a child with Marc.

Tegra believed needing a hysterectomy was punishment from God for her abortion. For the first time, she grieved the loss of her aborted child. "I felt tormented inside because I had never shared my abortion story with my husband," she said. "I felt a heavy weight on me because of what I was about to go through and because of what I had taken into my marriage." After surgery, Tegra went through a season of loneliness and deep depression. Problems surfaced in her marriage. With grief overwhelming her spirit, the Holy Spirit broke through and spoke to her heart. *You have not accepted My forgiveness for your abortion. You need to get some help.*

Tegra made an appointment with a Christian counselor. Questions that had been buried rose to the surface. Why hadn't her mother provided the comfort she needed when she went to her for help? She had grown up in a Christian household. She expected more and felt anger over her mother's actions. Why hadn't she stopped her from getting an abortion? And why had they never talked about it since? It was as if Tegra's abortion never happened. For healing to take place in her heart, she needed to be honest with her mother.

"I knew one day we would have this conversation," Tegra's mom said as they sat at the dining room table. She purposely had not brought up the subject until Tegra was ready to talk. "I did the best I could for you. I wanted to be there for you. You asked me to take you, and that's what I did for you." Regrets had not been limited to Tegra's heart alone. Her mother hadn't considered this abortion as the loss of her own grandchild. Reality struck hard as she contemplated her participation in the act of ending her grandchild's life. She broke down as Tegra shared that she harbored no more anger or judgment in her heart. Tears came freely. Forgiveness was released, and healing took place in their relationship.

Now it was time to come clean with her husband. As she confessed her abortion to Marc, compassion took over his heart. He prayed over her like never before. His prayer—and his acceptance of Tegra—broke the shame and condemnation that had overshadowed her life. Intimacy was restored.

As Tegra learned about the emotional and spiritual wounds caused by abortion, she was impressed with the importance of giving her baby a name. She entered into a time of prayer. The Lord showed her in a vision that her baby had been a girl. The Holy Spirit impressed her heart with the name for her baby, Or'el, a Hebrew name meaning "light of God."

After the hysterectomy Tegra and Marc shifted their focus as they sought to become parents in other ways. Through adoption, God had chosen them to be the parents of Rah'el, a six-week-old baby girl living in an Ethiopian orphanage. While in the United States waiting for their daughter to come home, Rah'el died through a tragic act of negligence. The news came as a shock, and a deep-seated feeling of regret came over Tegra for aborting her first baby. She thought she was cursed. Although she was a solid Christian, deeply rooted in the Word, active in ministry, and in a strong marriage, she entered into an even deeper depression. "I felt the enemy was trying to take control of my thoughts and was condemning me." Steeped in sadness and regret, she thought, *If I wouldn't have aborted Or'el, I wouldn't be here in this place.*

God delivered her from deep anger, resentment, and hatred toward the orphanage director whose negligence had led to her baby's death. Once again, the Holy Spirit spoke to her heart and identified her path for healing. *You will apologize to this man for the feelings you had and let him know how I delivered you from these feelings. You will be able to love on him. You will be able to pray with him. You will be able to forgive him.* Tegra and Marc went back to Ethiopia and asked forgiveness from the director of the orphanage. It was a time of cleansing. The spirits of depression, regret, and condemnation no longer had a hold on her heart.

Still childless, Tegra clung to Luke 1:45 for comfort: "Blessed is she who believed, for there will be a fulfillment of those things which were told her from the Lord." She wasn't cursed; she would be a mother. "We would be able to be parents, no matter what it looked like," she said. The following year, Tegra and Marc received a referral for the adoption of their Ethiopian son, Yakob. Their ten-year journey to becoming parents was soon fulfilled. Today Yakob is a healthy and active five-year-old who keeps his parents on their toes and fills their lives with joy. "God is so faithful," Tegra said. "He gave me beauty for ashes." His Word did not return void.

Tegra suffered for years under the weight of regret, condemnation, shame, and a feeling of unworthiness that had kept her from her dreams. When she crossed to the other side of abortion, she was able to dream again with purpose and vision. Tegra wants everyone who suffers from abortion and miscarriage to walk in victory and to be the people God created them to be. "It will take courage," she says. "Intercessory prayer is critical. But freedom is infectious. He will make you new."

The Lord led Tegra to establish an abortion-recovery ministry, No Longer Bound, for men and women who are hurting from the pain of abortion and miscarriage. Tegra encourages everyone with the truth that God is not a God who lies. "Whatever Scripture you are standing on, you can trust that word," she says. "There is hope in Christ. Don't give up. He's going to encourage you. He's going to give you what you need through every season. It may seem challenging. It may seem like it's not going to happen for you. Just keep holding on to His word."

Comfort

I, even I, **AM HE** WHO *comforts* YOU.

ISAIAH 51:12 NKJV

Let Love In

Endless love beyond measurement that transcends our understanding—
this extravagant love pours into you until you are filled to overflowing
with the fullness of God!
—Ephesians 3:19

HOW DEEP IS THE FATHER'S LOVE FOR YOU—how vast it is beyond all measure.

This love can never be fully understood by the human mind. Love must be encountered and experienced because it is an ongoing process that will continue to unfold before you all the days of your life.

Unwrap love like a gift. Let love wash over you and heal your pain, your disappointments, your sorrow. Let love anchor your soul. Let love calm your storm.

Let love in.

PAUSE IN REFLECTION
Quiet your heart

How receptive are you to the love of God? Is it easy to receive? Or do regret, guilt, and shame haunt your heart, creating barriers that are difficult to overcome?

Choose to believe His words over your feelings. Let His love wash over your heart anew as you fix your eyes on Him. Listen to His heart of love for you now.

PAUSE IN GOD'S PRESENCE

Listen for His voice

_____

_____

_____

_____

_____

_____

_____

_____

_____

_____

_____

_____

_____

_____

_____

_____

_____

_____

_____

Now may the Lord Jesus Christ and our Father God, who loved us and in his wonderful grace gave us eternal comfort and a beautiful hope that cannot fail, encourage your hearts, and inspire you with strength to always do and speak what is good and beautiful in his eyes.
—2 THESSALONIANS 2:16-17

DAY 26

Fix Your Eyes

Your eyes will see the King in His beauty.
—Isaiah 33:17 TLV

I LOVE YOU WITH ALL I AM. I meet with you when you come to Me—every time, without fail. I long to receive your heart of worship and love.

Press in for breakthroughs as you pull down the strongholds in your heart. Declare My purposes. Exalt My name. Lift Me up over the circumstances in your life, keeping your eyes firmly fixed on Me. This is so important, for when your eyes fail, your heart is quick to follow.

Focus on Me with your steady gaze. I am here.

PAUSE IN REFLECTION

Quiet your heart

Is regret a stronghold you continue to battle? What other breakthroughs are needed in your life?

Trust that the Lord has victory for you. Fix your eyes on His promises as you come into His presence with expectation and hope. Rest in the comfort He alone can give.

PAUSE IN GOD'S PRESENCE

Listen for His voice

*In all of my affliction I find great comfort in your promises,
for they have kept me alive!*
—Psalm 119:50

Expect My Answer

In the day of my trouble I will call upon You, for You will answer me.
—PSALM 86:7 NKJV

WHEN YOU CALL ON ME IN FAITH, you can expect My answer.

When you are in distress, I will not leave you feeling abandoned or alone. In those moments I am as close as your breath, whispered in the prayer of your heart. I am near to the brokenhearted, and I save those who are crushed in spirit.

Hold onto this word in your time of need. Call on Me, and I will answer you.

PAUSE IN REFLECTION

Quiet your heart

Do you struggle to believe God will answer you when you call to Him? Does past sin prevent you from reaching out to Him in faith for your needs? Do feelings of abandonment outweigh His promises that He will never leave you or forsake you?

What steps will you take to center your heart to trust His promises over your feelings? Write them down.

PAUSE IN GOD'S PRESENCE

Listen for His voice

_____
_____
_____
_____
_____
_____
_____
_____
_____
_____
_____
_____
_____
_____
_____
_____
_____
_____
_____
_____

*Lord, you know and understand all the hopes of the humble and will
hear their cries and comfort their hearts, helping them all!*
—Psalm 10:17

With You Always

And remember! I am with you always, even to the end of the age.
—Matthew 28:20 TLV

I AM WITH YOU ALWAYS. Always. Whether you feel worthy or not, and whether you have chosen well or not.

Consider the example of Martha. She busied herself with the cares of the world, distracted from what was most important. Where was I? Just a few steps away. I was near to her.

I am near to you too. As you draw close to Me, I will draw close to you. Keep your heart in tune with Mine.

PAUSE IN REFLECTION

Quiet your heart

Are there barriers or distractions in your life that prevent you from experiencing the joy of God's presence?

Read Psalm 139:7–12. Invite the Holy Spirit to show you His plan for overcoming these obstacles in your way. What do you think of these obstacles now?

PAUSE IN GOD'S PRESENCE

Listen for His voice

*Yet, in spite of all this, you comfort me by your counsel;
you draw me closer to you.*
—Psalm 73:23

Release Your Cares

This is my comfort in my affliction, that your promise gives me life.
—Psalm 119:50 esv

EVEN IN THE MOST DIFFICULT SITUATIONS OF LIFE, pain that you experience can be lessened when you allow Me to carry your burdens.

This does not mean you close your eyes to the reality of your situation, but rather acknowledge that you are not alone. You are seen and you are loved. I care about the cares of your heart as much as I care about you in the entirety of your body, soul, and spirit.

Release the cares you hold into My capable hands, exchanging them for the promises I have given. What promise is most meaningful to you in this situation you face?

Hold on in faith that My promise will be fulfilled for you.

PAUSE IN REFLECTION

Quiet your heart

You are not alone. Do these words resonate with your heart, or are there burdens you continue to carry in your own strength? What will it take for you to release these cares to the Lord? Do you believe He will help you?

Find His promise for you today.

PAUSE IN GOD'S PRESENCE

Listen for His voice

Whenever my busy thoughts were out of control, the soothing comfort of your presence calmed me down and overwhelmed me with delight.
—PSALM 94:19

Put on Peace

You're my place of quiet retreat, and your wrap-around presence
becomes my shield as I wrap myself in your word!
—PSALM 119:114

COME INTO MY PRESENCE. *Breathe.* If you are feeling anxiety of any kind, you have stepped away from My covenant of peace. Let My peace return to you now.

Release all the anxiety and cares of your heart. You put on pressure when you should put on peace. Let My wrap-around presence calm you from the inside out. Feel My presence. Focus on the one thing that is needful. Do that. The rest will fall into place.

I am with you. If I can hold the universe in place, I can certainly hold the cares of your heart and make your way smooth.

PAUSE IN REFLECTION

Quiet your heart

Does regret cause anxiety that grips your heart and won't let go? Do you put on pressure when you need to put on peace?

Read Psalm 29:11. Receive His blessing of peace into your heart.

PAUSE IN GOD'S PRESENCE

Listen for His voice

_____

_____

_____

_____

_____

_____

_____

_____

_____

_____

_____

_____

_____

_____

_____

_____

_____

_____

_____

Lord, even when your path takes me through the valley of deepest darkness, fear will never conquer me, for you already have! You remain close to me and lead me through it all the way. Your authority is my strength and my peace. The comfort of your love takes away my fear. I'll never be lonely, for you are near.
—Psalm 23:4

DAY 31

All You Need

God's glory is all around me! His wrap-around presence is all I need.
—PSALM 62:7

I FILL YOU WITH ALL YOU NEED. When you are worried, I fill you with peace. When you are discouraged, I fill you with hope. When you are fearful, I fill you with courage. When you are offended, I fill you with love. When you are in doubt, I fill you with faith and trust in Me. When you are weak, I fill you with My strength.

What do you need from Me today? This question goes beyond your wants and reaches the core of what you need. Simply ask.

PAUSE IN REFLECTION

Quiet your heart

Do you agree God will fill you with all you need? His supply will never run out.

Give Him the regrets of your past as you entrust Him with all your pain. Believe in His love for you.

PAUSE IN GOD'S PRESENCE

Listen for His voice

_____
_____
_____
_____
_____
_____
_____
_____
_____
_____
_____
_____
_____
_____
_____
_____
_____
_____

*I am contending for you that your hearts will be wrapped in the
comfort of heaven and woven together into love's fabric.
This will give you access to all the riches of God as you
experience the revelation of God's great mystery—Christ.*
—Colossians 2:2

In Silence

I am standing in absolute stillness, silent before the one I love.
—Psalm 62:5

IN SILENCE, YOU FIND ME.

Silence is a time to clear away all the distractions that hold you captive. Silence requires that you are intentional to direct all your attention toward Me as it brings you into a place of focused expectancy.

In the stillness of your soul, My glory is revealed. In this quiet place, you will hear My voice and experience My fullness.

Silence is an act of worship. Practice stillness often.

PAUSE IN REFLECTION

Quiet your heart

Is it difficult for you to quiet your heart? What are the distractions that steal your focus? Internal distractions can be more disruptive than external distractions.

Ask the Lord to help you center your heart on Him. Hear His words of life.

PAUSE IN GOD'S PRESENCE

Listen for His voice

Look how much encouragement you've found in your relationship with the Anointed One! You are filled to overflowing with his comforting love. You have experienced a deepening friendship with the Holy Spirit and have felt his tender affection and mercy.
—Philippians 2:1

SECTION V

From

Depression
to Hope

I'm slipping away and on the verge of a breakdown,
with nothing but sorrow and sighing.
—PSALM 38:17

EARLY IN HER CHILDHOOD, Pam was introduced to a life filled with heartbreak, trauma, and abuse. Born in 1973—the year abortion became legal—she narrowly escaped becoming an abortion statistic herself when her fifteen-year-old mother sought to terminate Pam's life while she was still in the womb. Instead, Pam's grandfather intervened and offered his home in Alabama as a refuge for her parents, a place where they could live together and raise their baby.

By the time Pam's mother turned twenty-four, she was married with four young children under her care, but Pam's home life was anything but stable. In her first eight years of life, Pam's family shuttled between twenty different homes. Inside their walls, life was chaotic, disorderly, and violent. Though Pam was spared from physical abuse, her father often beat her mother and left Pam to bathe her battered mom and care for her wounds. Roles were reversed as her mother became childlike, compelling Pam to become motherly. Violence rapidly reached its tipping point. Pam's father brutally beat his young wife to death and was sentenced to fifty years in prison, leaving his children without a mother or a father to care for them. With no other option available, the children were sent away to a foster home where they could stay together as a family. Fear and anxiety gripped Pam's heart and wouldn't let go.

Her new foster parents made it clear that Pam was responsible as protector and caretaker for her siblings. Two weeks after they arrived, Pam was alone with her five-month-old baby sister. When Pam wasn't looking, the baby rolled over and fell to the floor. Pam's failure to execute her duties to perfection infuriated her foster father. He lashed out at Pam, beating her severely as he whipped her with his belt, leaving her traumatized and in shock. Pam soldiered on as best she could, but the weight of responsibility crushed her with a burden of guilt she couldn't bear. She was eight years old.

Pam suffered a gamut of abuse at the hands of those who were entrusted with her care. Physical, emotional, and sexual assault were constant occurrences. Her foster mother despised her when Pam became "the other woman," the victim of her husband's sexual sin. Pain led Pam to alcohol, where addiction grabbed hold early—by eleven, her drinking was out of control. "I thought I was doomed to hell," Pam said. "I lived a hopeless life." No one told her about Jesus. She didn't know of His saving grace and mercy—or that a relationship with Him was possible.

Once she graduated high school, Pam ran away from her foster home. After ten years of torment, she gained the courage to inform the authorities of the abuse she had suffered. When the trial for her foster father began, Pam attempted suicide. His conviction and incarceration brought Pam freedom and a sense of empowerment, but she still wasn't healed. As time passed, Pam's mental anguish increased, and she made several other attempts to kill herself. A doctor diagnosed Pam with bipolar disorder and prescribed medications with the warning she would have to take these pills for the rest of her life.

Pam slipped into a lifestyle of promiscuity as rebellion filled her heart. "I was a slave to sin," she said. At nineteen, she joined the army and learned how to drink *really* well—and her dependency on alcohol increased. Pam married a fellow recruit and became pregnant. Her husband was elated with the news, but Pam felt differently. "I never wanted to be a mom," Pam said. She never thought she could be a *good* mom, because she had no foundation for motherhood. She believed a lie that said she was bad, with nothing to offer—but that was not true. She offered her baby a chance at life.

During her pregnancy, Pam stopped drinking and smoking, but she continued to exert herself in the intense physical demands as required by the army. This exertion caused Pam to go into premature labor, and she gave birth to her son nine weeks early. "When they gave him to me to hold, I had no connection with him," she said. Her mothering instincts were impaired. Her baby was placed in the NICU, which made bonding even more difficult. Postpartum depression darkened her mind. She struggled to take care of their child when she couldn't even take care of herself. Pam and her husband divorced when their son was a year old, and she relinquished all parental rights. Her ex-husband later remarried and raised their son in a loving home environment.

The following year Pam met Roger, the man who would one day become her husband. Before long, she became pregnant with his child and left her position with the army. On the day of her daughter's birth, Pam's heart changed. "It was as if I had known love for the first time in my life," she said. Pam still had no idea what to do, but her mothering instincts were different. She wanted to care for her baby and protect her. She was empowered with purpose—but her newfound joy in motherhood was not enough to stop her addictions. Four years after her daughter's birth, her addictions were as strong as ever. "I was using methamphetamines, opiates, snorting cocaine, smoking crack, and drinking alcohol—all while maintaining a job," she said. Pam created excuses to push Roger away. "I didn't feel worthy. I didn't feel deserving. If he knew everything about me, he wouldn't stay," she said. Roger wised up. If he remained in this relationship, it wouldn't end well, as addiction was active in his life too. Roger left, but he never stopped caring for her. Pam became a single parent to raise their daughter on her own.

Her life spiraled downward as she spun back to a lifestyle of promiscuity. She became pregnant again, only this time she didn't know who the father was. Unstable with no one to depend on, Pam asked everyone she knew—everyone she *trusted*—for guidance. Her aunts, uncles, friends, and coworkers all had the same advice. "Oh, Pam, you *can't* have this baby. You can't even take care of yourself!" Every door she opened to keep her baby was shut with the words *you can't*.

There was no voice of truth in her life.

Somehow, the idea of an abortion grabbed hold of her heart and became the only option she thought she had. "I felt like an animal backed into a corner," she said. "I felt like I had no choice." During this time, Pam's father was released from prison on parole after serving twenty years of his sentence. Though she couldn't explain it, the grace of God was on her life to be a good forgiver—and she believed her father deserved another chance. She chose to help him reconcile with society, and she welcomed him back into her life.

Several weeks later her dad performed his first fatherly duty and escorted her to the clinic for her abortion. They arrived to the clinic without fanfare. No one was there to stop her from entering—no protestors *and* no advocates for life. The clinic evoked a welcoming sense of home, with its cozy waiting area filled with people. Pam looked at the other girls in the room, laughing and giggling among themselves. *What is wrong with these people?* she wondered. And then she realized she was one of them. A battle raged inside her.

What am I doing? she questioned. *Why am I here?* She knew she wasn't making the best decision of her life—but she didn't think her choice was *wrong*. No one had provided counsel about her decision to end the life of the baby in her womb. At the clinic, it was assumed she had made her choice, and they weren't about to change her mind.

Pam was taken to the procedure room and given intravenous sedation. She had experience as a laboratory technician and had given birth to two children without an epidural. She wasn't squeamish and could tolerate pain, but when the doctor started the procedure, she tensed. She was fourteen weeks along and felt the pain and pressure. "No one comforted me or held my hand," she said. Before she knew it, her abortion was over.

In the recovery room, a few other girls lay back in recliners, relaxed. Pam could see that the medication was working for them. However, it was not working for *her*. She didn't feel well. Even with her high pain tolerance, the sensation radiating from her abdomen was severe, and she knew something was wrong. Pam stood and felt liquid pour down her body. "It was like something popped," she said. She made her way to the restroom, where she discovered blood. She pulled the cord to notify the nurses. When they came to help, they were alarmed. "Oh God, what did you do?" they asked.

The nurses reacted in fear as they put Pam on a gurney and wheeled her down the hallway before leaving her alone by the back door. Searing pain kept her in anguish. As she lay there bleeding and alone, her father continued to wait for her. No one informed him that Pam was in trouble, that her uterus had been perforated during the abortion procedure. When an ambulance arrived at the back of the clinic, Pam's father was finally brought to her, and he accompanied her on the ride to the emergency room. At the hospital the staff was attentive and caring, and

Pam sensed compassion from these workers. She spent the night in the hospital while her body began to heal.

On Tuesday, September 11, 2001, Pam returned to work. As she filed paperwork and processed insurance claims with her coworkers, they listened to the morning television news program. It was their normal Tuesday routine—but nothing was routine about that day. Together they watched the hijacked planes fly into the Twin Towers. Her personal tragedy was dwarfed by the catastrophe that swept over the nation. She shoved her abortion experience down deep inside her heart. Though she repressed thoughts of her abortion, she never forgot her baby's due date. "You can abort your baby," Pam said, "but you can never get rid of the *memory* of your baby."

Pam became highly addicted to the opiates prescribed for her following her abortion. Her addiction escalated over the next two years—and her life fell apart. She attempted suicide again. She didn't realize her abortion was at the root of these problems. When she was at her lowest point, God opened the door for her healing journey to begin. Pam attended Alcoholics Anonymous meetings, where she first called out to God in prayer. When she served the needs of others, her heart changed. She gave up drugs. On April 26, 2004, she became sober—and she has not turned back. A short time after reaching sobriety, Pam reunited with Roger, and they married. It wasn't long before they welcomed another baby girl into their family.

Over the next five years, Pam lived without dependency on drugs or alcohol. However, she couldn't understand why she found it so difficult to manage her life. Disorder, dysfunction, and a lack of trust prevailed, and the pain of her past resurfaced continually. She moved to Texas with her husband and daughters, where a family member invited them to church. Pam surrendered her life to Christ, and her transformation continued to unfold. At an "Encounter God" weekend sponsored by her church, Pam was touched by the powerful presence of God. She called on the name of Jesus, and His Spirit filled her heart. "He *changed* me," she said. "His Word changed me. A power rose up in me. I saw everything differently." When God changed her thoughts, her identity in Him was revealed.

Healing then wove its path through many of the broken pieces of her past.

Pam discovered she didn't have to live with despair. She learned how to live in victory and freedom by renouncing words that didn't bring life. "We can have the mind of Christ," she said. Pam returned to her doctor and received permission to discontinue her lifetime medications for bipolar disorder. She has been free from these medications—and free from mental pain and instability—for ten years now.

Today Pam and Roger have a loving, thriving marriage and are actively parenting their two beautiful daughters with joy. Pam's son, whom she'd relinquished as a baby, is now married with a fulfilling career in the military. Pam is a projects and client manager for And Then There Were None, Abby Johnson's pro-life organization that exists to help abortion workers leave the abortion industry. Pam also volunteers her time with the organization Sidewalk Advocates for Life. Together, Pam and Roger lead "The High Road to Recovery," a 12-step program they developed for those who desire to overcome addiction.

Pam shares words of comfort and hope for those who are struggling with the pain of depression: "If God could do it for me—if He could love me the way that He's loved me—don't think for one moment that He's not thinking of you too. You do not have to believe the lies of the enemy. The Lord can change you," she says, "and He *will*."

Hope

Your future is
bright
and filled with a
LIVING **HOPE**
that will *never*
FADE AWAY.

~ PROVERBS 23:18 ~

The Time to Draw Near

Here's the one thing I crave from God, the one thing I seek above all else: I want the privilege of living with him every moment in his house, finding the sweet loveliness of his face, filled with awe, delighting in glory and grace. I want to live my life so close to him that he takes pleasure in my every prayer.
—Psalm 27:4

NOW IS NOT THE TIME TO LET YOUR MIND WANDER; it is the time to draw near. Come to Me for all you need.

What do you desire of Me today? Will you focus on the cares of your life, or will you direct your heart to look for Me? The cares of life compete for the attention of your heart, but if you make it your practice to seek Me first—to seek Me with focus, purpose, and intention—then I will care for all these other things that concern you and weigh you down.

Choose the better part today. Choose Me.

PAUSE IN REFLECTION

Quiet your heart

What cares of life are competing for the attention of your heart? Is it hard for you to direct your focus to God? Depression can cause difficulty in thinking, in focusing, and in making decisions. Realize the enemy's purpose is to steal, kill, and destroy—he creates separation in relationships, both with God and others the Lord has put in your life.

Overcome the objectives of the enemy of your soul. Go deeper with God. Seek Him now.

PAUSE IN GOD'S PRESENCE

Listen for His voice

_____
_____
_____
_____
_____
_____
_____
_____
_____
_____
_____
_____
_____
_____
_____
_____
_____
_____
_____
_____
_____

The Lord alone is our radiant hope and we trust in him with all our hearts. His wrap-around presence will strengthen us.
—PSALM 33:20

Peace in the Storm

And immediately Jesus stretched out His hand and caught him, and said to him, "O you of little faith, why did you doubt?"
—MATTHEW 14:31 NKJV

THIS IS YOUR STORM—these are your waves. Do not be like Peter, who let his great faith diminish into little faith because he became overwrought with the realities of the natural world. Do not fall back into worry or despair, but press in to the promises I have given you.

I am in front of you, standing on the water—defying all the natural laws of earth to demonstrate the supernatural laws of heaven. I extend My hand to you. Will you have peace in the storm? Walk!

PAUSE IN REFLECTION

Quiet your heart

Does depression keep you trapped in a cycle of negativity? Is it difficult for you to take your eyes off of your natural circumstances? Trust that the Lord stands in front of you with His hand extended to pull you up.

What is one truth of His you can hold on to? Receive His peace in the middle of your storm.

PAUSE IN GOD'S PRESENCE

Listen for His voice

_____

_____

_____

_____

_____

_____

_____

_____

_____

_____

_____

_____

_____

_____

_____

_____

_____

_____

_____

Now may God, the inspiration and fountain of hope,
fill you to overflowing with uncontainable joy
and perfect peace as you trust in him.
—ROMANS 15:13

Hope Waits for You

So then, prepare your hearts and minds for action! Stay alert and fix your hope on the marvelous grace that is coming to you.
—1 PETER 1:13

FOCUS ON MY KINGDOM. Fix your hope on the reality that cannot be shaken, no matter what comes your way.

Hope heals disappointments from the past as it centers your heart on the realities of things to come. Hope heals hearts and unites faith with love. Hope is stronger than you know. Give hope the attention it deserves. Make room in your life for hope to grow. Raise your expectation to align with My promises.

Hope waits for you.

PAUSE IN REFLECTION

Quiet your heart

When was the last time you allowed hope into your heart? Does the thought of finding hope again seem hopeless? The Lord promises hope for your future (see Jeremiah 29:11).

Raise your expectation as you focus on His heart of love for you. Ask Him to fill you with His hope for one area that causes you distress. He who promised is faithful.

PAUSE IN GOD'S PRESENCE

Listen for His voice

_____

_____

_____

_____

_____

_____

_____

_____

_____

_____

_____

_____

_____

_____

_____

_____

_____

_____

_____

*So now we must cling tightly to the hope that lives within us,
knowing that God always keeps his promises!*
—Hebrews 10:23

DAY 36

Always in Motion

Quiet your heart in his presence and pray;
keep hope alive as you long for God to come through for you.
—Psalm 37:7

IN TIMES when it seems like "nothing" is happening—no movement, no change in your circumstances, no outward display of growth—understand My purposes are always in motion.

Not everything is discernible with the naked eye. Microscopes and telescopes show the detailed perspective of the natural realm. In the same way, supernatural vision is released when you draw on the power of My Spirit to go deep and high. How do you enter into this level of discernment? You engage through the power of prayer.

Pray.

PAUSE IN REFLECTION
Quiet your heart

Is it difficult for you to discern the positive changes of growth taking place in your life? What changes can you make to see your situation with a renewed perspective? Romans 8:34 says that Jesus is at the right hand of God, interceding for you now.

Join your voice with His and pray in agreement with His heart.

PAUSE IN GOD'S PRESENCE

Listen for His voice

*Even in times of trouble we have a joyful confidence, knowing that our
pressures will develop in us patient endurance. And patient endurance will
refine our character, and proven character leads us back to hope.*
—ROMANS 5:3-4

Perseverance Brings Breakthrough

God's amazing grace has made me who I am! And his grace to me was not fruitless. In fact, I worked harder than all the rest, yet not in my own strength but God's, for his empowering grace is poured out upon me.
—1 CORINTHIANS 15:10

I AM TEACHING YOU PERSEVERANCE. Patience is brought to maturity when you learn to persevere for the release of My promises.

Breakthrough does not happen in a vacuum. Breakthrough is the tipping point when all your prayers, agreements, and tangible demonstrations of faith converge with My promises to shatter every objection, obstacle, and opposition that stand in the way.

Continue to persevere in hope. Keep your eyes on the focal point of My face, not on your earthly situations. As you walk this road of perseverance, My grace grows in your heart, and my empowering presence gives you strength.

PAUSE IN REFLECTION

Quiet your heart

Are you ready for a breakthrough in your life? Do you live with expectation that He will move on your behalf?

Settle the matter of God's love for you in your heart. Agree with His promises as His grace fills you with strength to endure. Breakthrough is on the way.

PAUSE IN GOD'S PRESENCE

Listen for His voice

*This is why I wait upon you, expecting your breakthrough,
for your word brings me hope.*
—Psalm 130:5

Transformed by Love

We have come into an intimate experience with God's love, and we
trust in the love he has for us. God is love! Those who are living in love
are living in God, and God lives through them.
—1 JOHN 4:16

EACH DAY YOU SET TIME to come into My presence, I transform you with My love. In My presence, your youth is restored, your energy revitalized, your soul renewed, and your spirit recharged. What a wonderful place to be!

I long to demonstrate how much I love you. My love cannot be contained in words alone–it spills out and overflows. When I consider you, My joy is immeasurable. I see your identity and destiny, and My heart explodes in joyful anticipation for what is to come.

You are chosen and cherished. My love for you has no limits. None.

PAUSE IN REFLECTION

Quiet your heart

You are loved with an everlasting love. Can you feel it? Or have your emotions shut down, making you unable to feel joy, sorrow, or the love of God?

Invite the Lord to touch these inner places of your heart that need His healing. Little by little, let Him transform your heart with His love.

PAUSE IN GOD'S PRESENCE

Listen for His voice

This hope is not a disappointing fantasy, because we can now experience the endless love of God cascading into our hearts through the Holy Spirit who lives in us!
—ROMANS 5:5

My Power Unleashed

That is why, for Christ's sake, I delight in weaknesses, in insults, in hardships, in persecutions, in difficulties. For when I am weak, then I am strong.
—2 Corinthians 12:10 niv

REMEMBER WHEN YOU FACE TRIALS, insults, or hardships, your focus needs to be on My power unleashed in you. Keep your focus where it belongs, and you take away strength from the enemy's camp. His purpose is to bring you into a place of despair, where you exchange My truth for a lie.

In your weakness, My power rests on you.

PAUSE IN REFLECTION

Quiet your heart

Day by day as you have come into the presence of the Lord, have you felt His strength flowing into your heart? Are you aware of His voice crushing the lies of the enemy that kept you in despair? Is there a renewal of hope?

Thank Him for His power that rests on you. Thank Him for His strengthening help.

PAUSE IN GOD'S PRESENCE

Listen for His voice

_____

_____

_____

_____

_____

_____

_____

_____

_____

_____

_____

_____

_____

_____

_____

_____

_____

_____

_____

_____

We pray that you would be energized with all his explosive power from the realm of his magnificent glory, filling you with great hope.
—Colossians 1:11

DAY 40

My Plans for You

"For I know the plans I have for you," declares the LORD, "plans to prosper you and not to harm you, plans to give you hope and a future."
—JEREMIAH 29:11 NIV

DO NOT THINK FOR A MOMENT that the life you have been living is the life you will always lead. I have plans for you that far exceed what you have even asked for or thought—and yet, My plans will resonate with the desires of your heart.

My plans are released as you walk in faith with Me, one step at a time. I will show you where to go, what to do, what to say.

PAUSE IN REFLECTION

Quiet your heart

Can you identify the desires of your heart, or are they buried deep within? Now is the time to dream again. Don't be afraid to write down your dreams.

Ask the Lord to show you His plans for you. His plans are to prosper you—to give you a future and a hope. Dream big!

PAUSE IN GOD'S PRESENCE

Listen for His voice

*Now faith brings our hopes into reality and becomes the foundation
needed to acquire the things we long for.*
—Hebrews 11:1

A Prayer for Life

Thank You, Lord, for releasing life over those who are walking on this journey of healing with You. Continue to strengthen them as they hold onto Your truth, crushing the lies of the enemy that have kept them bound. Give them courage to face their fears, knowing You are by their side. You will never leave them or abandon them. Wrap them in Your peace.

May they feel the comfort of Your love as You encounter them and fill them with Your powerful presence. Thank You that Your love breaks the chains of addiction and despair, bringing light to the darkness and infusing them with life. Give them confident assurance that the same Spirit who raised Christ Jesus from the dead now lives in them—and that in You, all things are possible!

By the power of Your Spirit, may they have boldness to forgive those who have hurt them, so they may return blessing to them instead. Bring restoration to relationships that have been fractured and broken. As they open their hearts to receive Your forgiveness, may Your love come in like a flood, filling them until they overflow.

Thank You that there is now no condemnation for those who are in Christ Jesus. Release a fresh understanding of renewed identity, destiny, and purpose into their hearts, as they release Your fragrance of life into the world around them. May nothing hold them back.

In the powerful name of Jesus, I pray this in faith and agreement with Your will. Amen!

Resources

Post-Abortion Healing, Counseling, and Care

And Then There Were None
888-570-5501
info@abortionworker.com
www.abortionworker.com

Amazing Love Healing Ministry
Reverend Dr. Sharon Lewis
941-404-1004
info@amazinglovehealing.com
www.amazinglovehealing.com

Care Net Pregnancy Centers
703-554-8734
info@care-net.org
www.care-net.org

Choose Grace International
Kay Lyn Carlson, LSW
804-835-6505
kaylyn@choosegrace.com
www.choosegrace.com

Concepts of Truth International
The national HELPLINE for abortion recovery
866-482-LIFE (5433)
www.internationalhelpline.org

No Longer Bound
Tegra Little
310-846-3227
nolongerbound@faithfamily.org
www.faithfulcentral.com/nolongerbound

Recovery Retreats and Workshops

No Longer Bound
Tegra Little
310-846-3227
nolongerbound@faithfamily.org
www.faithfulcentral.com/nolongerbound

Rachel's Vineyard
877-467-3463
assistant@rachelsvineyard.org
www.rachelsvineyard.org

Speakers Bureau

Abby Johnson
Author of *Unplanned* and *The Walls are Talking*
Topics: Abortion Healing, Abortion Industry, Adoption, Crisis Pregnancy, Pro-Life
www.ambassadorspeakers.com/speakers/unique/abby-johnson
abby@abbyjohnson.org
www.abbyjohnson.org

Annette Biggers
Testimony: From Grief to Joy
A Creative Change
Topics: Abortion Healing, Crisis Pregnancy, Adoption, Pro-Life
www.acreativechange.com

Michael Lombardo
Testimony: From Guilt to Forgiveness
Life Poured Out International
Author of *Immersed in His Glory*
Topics: Men and Abortion, Abortion Healing, Pro-Life
www.lifepouredoutintl.org

Kay Lyn Carlson, LSW
Testimony: From Shame to Grace
Choose Grace International
Topics: Abortion Healing, Crisis Pregnancy, Pro-Life
804-835-6505
kaylyn@choosegrace.com
www.choosegrace.com

Tegra Little

Testimony: From Regret to Comfort

No Longer Bound

Topics: Abortion Healing, Crisis Pregnancy, Men and Abortion, Pro-Life, Adoption

310-846-3227

nolongerbound@faithfamily.org

www.faithfulcentral.com/nolongerbound

Pam Whitehead

Testimony: From Depression to Hope

And Then There Were None

Topics: Pro-Life, Abortion Healing, Sidewalk Advocacy, Addiction Recovery, Sexual Abuse, Crisis Pregnancy

979-561-7285

pam@abortionworker.com

www.abortionworker.com

Reverend Dr. Sharon Lewis

Amazing Love Healing Ministry

Topics: Inner Healing

941-404-1004

info@amazinglovehealing.com

www.amazinglovehealing.com

Lorraine Marie Varela

Inspiring Faith International

Author of *Planned from the Start, Love in the Face of ISIS* and *Powerful Moments in the Presence of God*

Topics: Faith, Inner Healing, Pro-Life

hello@inspiringfaith.us

www.inspiringfaith.us

Order Information

To order additional copies of this book,
please visit www.redemption-press.com.

Bulk discounts available

Special ministry discounts apply to churches, crisis pregnancy
centers, post-abortion healing groups and counseling centers.

For details contact:
www.unplanned.com/devotional
www.redemption-press.com/planned-from-the-start

ROMANS 8:28 BOOKS

AN IMPRINT OF REDEMPTION PRESS